Brands We Know

LEGO

By Sara Green

Bellwether Media • Minneapolis, MN

Jump into the cockpit and take flight with *Pilot* books. Your journey will take you on high-energy adventures as you learn about all that is wild, weird, fascinating, and fun!

This edition first published in 2015 by Bellwether Media, Inc.

No part of this publication may be reproduced in whole or in part without written permission of the publisher.
For information regarding permission, write to Bellwether Media, Inc.,
Attention: Permissions Department,
5357 Penn Avenue South, Minneapolis, MN 55419.

Library of Congress Cataloging-in-Publication Data

Green, Sara, 1964-
  LEGO / by Sara Green.
     pages cm. -- (Pilot: Brands We Know)
  Includes bibliographical references and index.
   Summary: "Engaging images accompany information about the LEGO Group. The combination of high-interest subject matter and narrative text is intended for students in grades 3 through 7"-- Provided by publisher.
   Audience: 7-12.
   Audience: Grades 3-7.
   ISBN 978-1-62617-208-1 (hardcover : alk. paper)
   1. LEGO koncernen (Denmark)--History--Juvenile literature. 2. Toy industry--Denmark--Juvenile literature. 3. Toy industry--United States--Juvenile literature. 4. LEGO toys--History--Juvenile literature. I. Title.
   HD9993.T694L4434 2015
   338.7'688725--dc23
                   2014040189

Printed in the United States of America, North Mankato, MN.

Table of Contents

What Is the LEGO Brand?

LEGO products have delighted children and adults for generations. The LEGO System is a line of construction toys. It includes plastic bricks, **minifigures**, gears, and wheels. The LEGO **brand** is among the most respected toy brands on Earth. It is also famous for its games, movies, and theme parks.

Though the company **headquarters** are in Billund, Denmark, LEGO products are sold in more than 130 countries. They are popular for many reasons. LEGO elements come in a huge range of shapes and sizes. People **interlock** bricks to make buildings, vehicles, and countless other shapes. Each LEGO piece fits into any other piece. They are also easy to take apart. Playing with LEGO products allows people to be creative. Many children enjoy building LEGO structures with friends. They can plan designs and solve problems together while they play. LEGO products inspire people to use their imaginations!

By the Numbers

about
94
LEGO bricks for each
person in the world

about
5 billion
hours of LEGO fun
enjoyed by children
per year

about
1,750
LEGO elements
produced per
second in 2013

more than
5 billion
LEGO minifigures
produced through 2014

more than
915 million
ways to combine six 4x2
LEGO bricks

about
4,200
different
LEGO elements

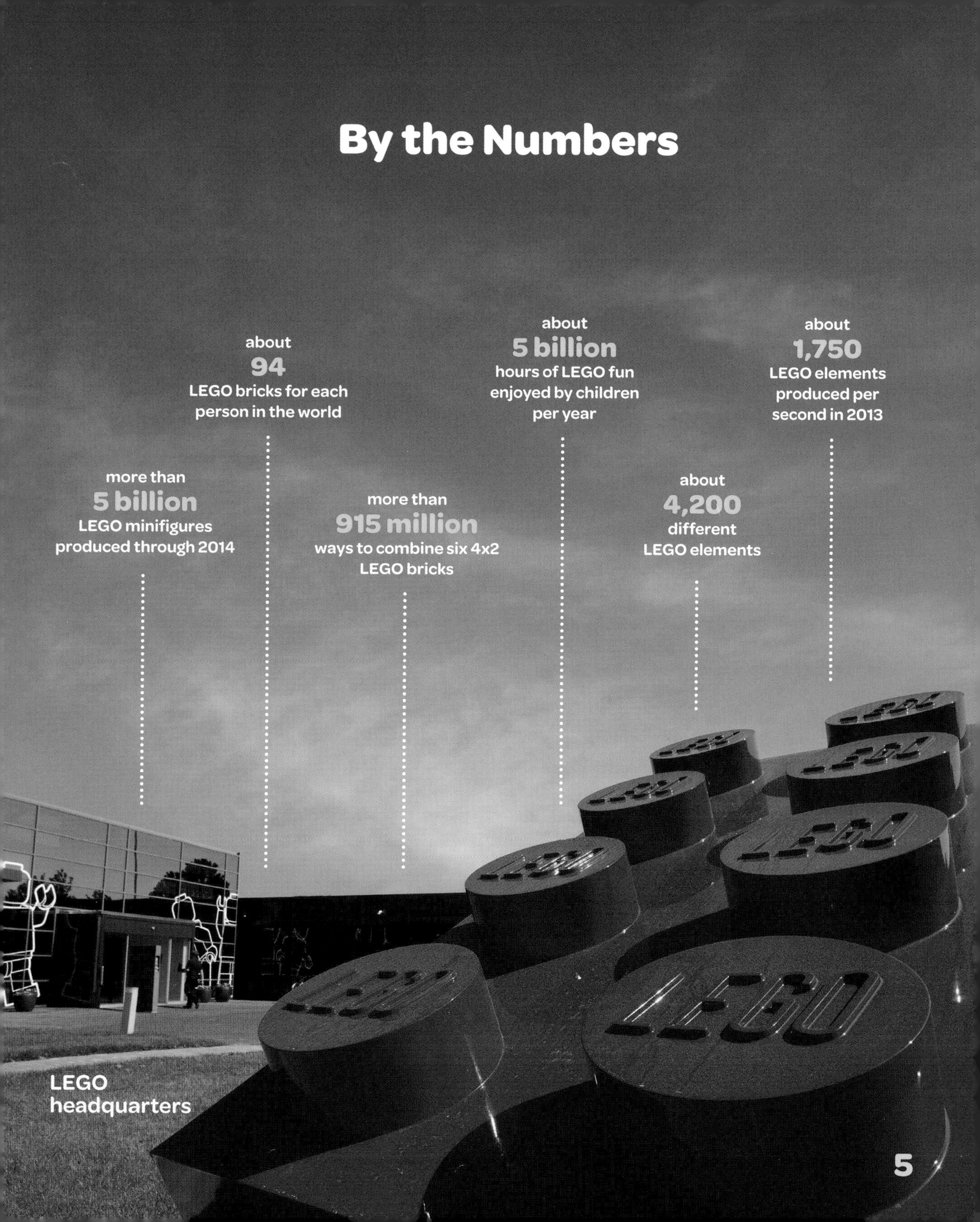

**LEGO
headquarters**

Ole Kirk Christiansen

The father of the LEGO brand is a man named Ole
Kirk Christiansen. He invented the first LEGO toys. Ole
was born on April 7, 1891, in a small village in Denmark.
As a child, he enjoyed carving figures out of wood. Later,
Ole trained to become a **carpenter**. In 1916, he bought a
carpentry shop in Billund, Denmark. There, he built homes
and furniture.

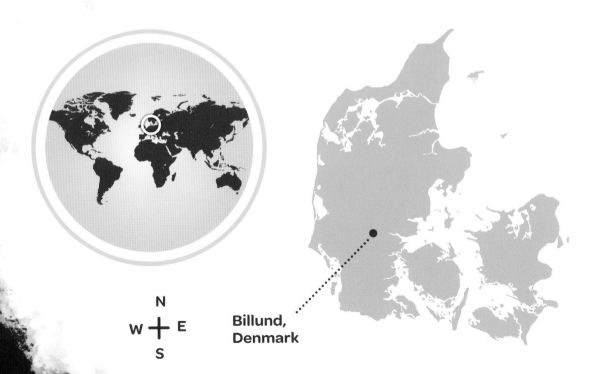

N
W ┼ E
S

**Billund,
Denmark**

Ole Kirk Christiansen

For many years, Ole's business was successful. Then the world experienced the **Great Depression**. People across the globe were left penniless. Ole's customers could no longer afford to buy houses or furniture. Ole had to **adapt** to keep his business running. He began to build less expensive items, such as wooden ironing boards, stools, and ladders. He also made wooden yo-yos, animals, and other toys. Customers loved the toys. They became his best-selling items. Soon, Ole decided to focus only on toys.

Only the best is good enough.

1930s-2010s tagline

In 1934, Ole decided to give his toy business a name. He asked the workers in his factory for ideas. However, Ole also had his own idea. He blended the Danish words *leg* and *godt* into the word "LEGO." The two words mean "play well." The name stuck. A few years later, Ole's son, Godtfred, started designing with his father. Now building LEGO toys was a family business.

In 1946, Ole made an important purchase. He bought a special machine that cast plastic into different shapes. Ole began to make toys with plastic. He made plastic rattles, cars, and trucks. He also created a set of small plastic bricks that snapped together easily. He called them LEGO **Automatic** Binding Bricks. In 1953, Ole shortened the name of his invention to simply LEGO bricks.

Automatic ·········
Binding Brick

The Growth of a Family Business

By then, Godtfred had become a leader at the company. He was proud of LEGO toys. However, he wanted children to be able to use them in more creative ways. In 1955, Godtfred introduced the "LEGO System of Play." This system included 28 LEGO sets and 8 toy vehicles. Each piece interlocked with pieces from other sets. Children could follow a set's directions and build what was on the box. They could also combine pieces from different sets and make up their own designs.

Children enjoyed the new LEGO system. However, the bricks did not always stick together tightly. In 1957, Godtfred invented a new way of linking the bricks. Each brick had **studs** on top. Godtfred added tubes to the bottoms. With the tubes, the bricks snapped together and held tight. They unsnapped easily, too. A year later, Godtfred filed a **patent** for this clever design.

Around the World
In 2013, enough LEGO bricks were made to circle the world more than 20 times!

How Many Bricks?

The Taj Mahal
the largest LEGO set:
more than 5,900

LEGOLAND
in Billund, Denmark:
more than 60 million

**The world's tallest
LEGO tower**
in Budapest, Hungary:
more than 450,000

LEGO Mona Lisa
by artist Nathan Sawaya:
4,573

The 1960s saw a huge growth in sales of LEGO products. The first LEGO sets went on sale in the United States in 1961. Soon, they were being sold throughout the world. In 1969, DUPLO bricks were introduced for young children. They are larger and wider than the original LEGO bricks. This makes DUPLO bricks safer and easier for young children to use.

LEGOLAND

The first LEGOLAND theme park opened in Billund in 1968. Today, there are six other LEGOLAND parks in the world. Visitors enjoy rides, life-size LEGO brick models, and places to build their own creations.

Castle

Pirate

Ninjago

In 1974, LEGO sets began to include figures. The first figures did not have arms or faces. In 1978, the modern minifigure, or minifig, was introduced. Over time, LEGO minifigs grew to have thousands of different looks. Children enjoyed **role-playing** with pirates, athletes, movie characters, and many other minifigs. LEGO sets with themes also started becoming popular in the late 1970s. The first themed sets were Town, Castle, and Space. Later sets included Pirate and Ninjago.

Today, the LEGO Group is still owned by the same family. The company continues to make exciting products. Older children challenge themselves with Technic sets. Both adults and children enjoy building robots with MINDSTORMS kits. These robots can be programmed to walk, talk, and think. Themed LEGO sets are still extremely successful. Many are based on famous movies and stories. *Star Wars*, Marvel Super Heroes, and Disney Princesses are all part of the LEGO universe.

MINDSTORMS robot

Star Wars

Disney Princess Merida

Marvel Super Heroes

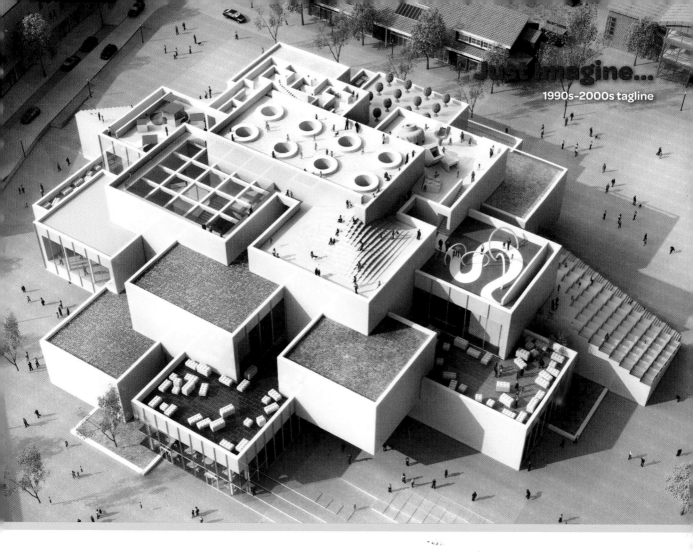

Soon, LEGO fans will be able to visit the LEGO House. This center is being built in Billund. It will be shaped like a stack of LEGO bricks. Visitors will be able to play with LEGO products and learn about LEGO history. They can relax in gardens and a café. There will even be a gift shop with LEGO **souvenirs**.

FIRST LEGO League

The LEGO Group is best known for its toys. However, the company also helps kids learn about science. It works with a science and technology program called FIRST. In 1998, FIRST began holding a yearly competition. It is called FIRST LEGO League, or FLL. Students work in small teams with adult coaches. They research a theme and complete a project related to it. Past themes include Mission Mars and Climate Connections. Teams also use LEGO MINDSTORMS kits to build and program robots.

Thousands of teams from around the world participate in FLL competitions. Awards are given for best project and for teamwork. Team members must show judges that they work well together. They must **cooperate** and respect one another. Teams are also judged on their robots. The robots perform a series of tasks in front of judges. Design and performance are two robot award categories.

A LEGO In Space

In 2001, Jitter became the first LEGO MINDSTORMS robot to go into space. Jitter was sent to the International Space Station. Its job was to collect trash.

Builders of tomorrow

2010s tagline

17

The LEGO Foundation

In 1986, Godtfred and his wife, Edith, started the LEGO **Foundation**. Their goal was to give LEGO products to needy children around the world. Today the foundation's main purpose is to help less fortunate children learn through play. The foundation works with other **charitable** organizations around the world. Together, they provide money and LEGO sets to children and schools in poor communities in many countries.

The LEGO Foundation at the United Nations

Create the impossible

2000s tagline

One project helps children who are **refugees**. In 2014, the LEGO Foundation donated $3 million to the United Nations refugee program. The money helps more than 200,000 children in twelve countries. Many of them have not been able to attend school. The donation is being used to build schools and train teachers in refugee camps. The foundation also donated LEGO products to the schools. Teachers use them to teach math, science, and other skills to the children. The LEGO Foundation is proud to help build a better future for children.

LEGO Timeline

1891
Ole Kirk Christiansen
is born near Filskov,
Denmark, on April 7

1949
The first Automatic
Binding Bricks are made

1957
Godtfred invents
a new way of
interlocking the
bricks with tubes
and studs

1946
Ole buys a plastic injection
molding machine

1920
Godtfred Kirk Christiansen
is born in Billund on July 8

1916
Ole opens a carpentry
shop in Billund, Denmark

1934
Ole gives his toy
business the
LEGO name

1955
Godtfred introduces
the "LEGO System
of Play"

1958
Ole passes away
and Godtfred
takes charge

1968
The first LEGOLAND
theme park opens
in Billund

1986
Godtfred and his wife, Edith,
start the LEGO Foundation

2000
The British Association
of Toy Retailers names
LEGO bricks the
"Toy of the Century"

2006
MINDSTORMS NXT robot
sets are launched

1995
Godtfred passes
away on July 13

2014
The LEGO Movie
plays in theaters

1969
The LEGO DUPLO
series is introduced

1998
LEGO joins
the National Toy
Hall of Fame

Glossary

adapt—to adjust to different conditions

automatic—happening with no help from a person

brand—a category of products all made by the same company

carpenter—a person who builds or repairs wooden structures

charitable—helping others in need

cooperate—to work with others to achieve a goal

foundation—an institution that provides funds to charitable organizations

Great Depression—a time in world history when many countries experienced economic crisis; the Great Depression began in 1929 and lasted through the 1930s.

headquarters—a company's main office

interlock—to lock together

minifigures—LEGO figurines

patent—an official document that says an inventor is the only person who can make or sell his or her invention

refugees—people who flee their countries to escape war or violence

role-playing—pretending to be a character

souvenirs—things that are reminders of a place

studs—small knobs

To Learn More

AT THE LIBRARY

Hirschmann, Kris. *LEGO Toys*. Chicago, Ill.: Norwood House Press, 2009.

Lipkowitz, Daniel. *The LEGO Ideas Book: Unlock Your Imagination*. New York, N.Y.: DK, 2011.

Moss, Jenny. *How Robots Work*. North Mankato, Minn.: Capstone Press, 2013.

ON THE WEB

Learning more about LEGO is as easy as 1, 2, 3.

1. Go to www.factsurfer.com.

2. Enter "LEGO" into the search box.

3. Click the "Surf" button and you will see a list of related web sites.

With factsurfer.com, finding more information is just a click away.

Index